Tongue Twisters

+300 funny, tricky, tough for kids and adults

Adam Smith

Tongue Twisters
Copyright © 2017 by Adam Smith.

All rights reserved. Printed in the United States of America. No part of this book may be used or reproduced in any manner whatsoever without written permission except in the case of brief quotations em- bodied in critical articles or reviews.
This book is a work of fiction. Names, characters, businesses, organizations, places, events and incidents either are the product of the author's imagination or are used fictitiously. Any resemblance to actual persons, living or dead, events, or locales is entirely coincidental.

For information contact :book_author@yahoo.com

Book and Cover design by Ploae
ISBN:9781545276204

First Edition: April 2017

A tongue-twister is a phrase that is designed to be difficult to **articulate** properly, and can be used as a type of spoken (or sung) **word game**. Some tongue-twisters produce results that are humorous (or humorously vulgar) when they are mispronounced, while others simply rely on the confusion and mistakes of the speaker for their amusement value.

Tongue-twisters may rely on rapid alternation between similar but distinct **phonemes** (e.g., s [s] and sh), combining two different alternation patterns, familiar constructs in **loanwords**, or other features of a spoken language in order to be difficult to articulate. For example, the following sentence was claimed as "the most difficult of common English-language tongue-twisters" by **William Poundstone**.

"The seething sea ceaseth and thus the seething sea sufficeth us."

Get Ready!

Read as fast as you can!

She sells seashells on the seashore.

Please put this porcupine in your pants.

The crowd of clumsy clowns crushed the king's crown.

The detective discovered the deadly dagger in Dad's dirty diapers.

The tiny teacher (on tippytoes) tamed the terrible T-Rex by tickling its tummy.

Noisy boys enjoy noisy toys, but noisy boys enjoying noisy toys are annoying.

The fat farmer's five filthy fingers fed the ferocious ferret french fries.

Greedy Grandpa grabbed Grandma's greasy grubs.

The peppy puppy the prince presented the princess produced piles of poop in the palace.

"You're making a mistake marrying that monster!"

moaned the mummy's mother.

The hippos heard the hunter's hiccups and hurried home to hide.

The big, bumbling bear burned his butt baking bread.

Six stinky skunks sprayed Santa's sleigh.

"Yellow yarn is yummy!" yelled the young yak.

The twins took the toilet and tiptoed toward town to try trading it for toys.

My sister's shop sells shoes for sheep.

Firefighters found Father frowning from a funny fever and farting fierce flames.

The nervous nurse had another nasty nosebleed and needed nine napkins for her nostrils.

"Juicy!" joked the janitor, his jaws on the jiggling jellyfish. 20. If eight great apes ate eighty-eight grapes, guess how many grapes each great ape ate.

The little lambs, licking lollipops, went leaping and laughing into the lava.

When the wizard winked and waved his wand, the wars of the world went away.

Mix a box of mixed

Tongue Twisters

biscuits with a boxed biscuit mixer.
••••••••••••••••••••••

A proper copper coffee pot.
••••••••••••••••••••••

I saw Esau sitting on a seesaw. Esau, he saw me.
••••••••••••••••••••••

Toy boat. Toy boat. Toy boat.
••••••••••••••••••••••

Lovely lemon liniment.
••••••••••••••••••••••

Six thick thistle sticks. Six thick thistles stick.
••••••••••••••••••••••

Good blood, bad blood. (x3)
••••••••••••••••••••••

Three free throws. (x3)
••••••••••••••••••••••

The instinct of an extinct insect stinks.
••••••••••••••••••••••

Which wristwatches are Swiss wristwatches?
••••••••••••••••••••••

Peter Piper picked a peck of pickled peppers.
A peck of pickled peppers Peter Piper picked.
If Peter Piper picked a peck of pickled peppers,
Where's the peck of pickled peppers Peter Piper picked?
••••••••••••••••••••••

The greedy Greek geek agreed.
••••••••••••••••••••••

Frozen Floyd flicks fat fleas for a fixed flat fee.
••••••••••••••••••••••

Many an anemone sees an enemy anemone.
••••••••••••••••••••••

An inchworm inches on ivy that itches.
••••••••••••••••••••••

Nope, an antelope can't

elope with a cantelope.
■■■■■■■■■■■■■■■■■■■■■

"Two tried" and "True tied".(x3)
■■■■■■■■■■■■■■■■■■■■■

Three free fleas flew freely through the flu.
■■■■■■■■■■■■■■■■■■■■■

The CEO's colleagues trusted those successful clients although their results weren't less than lumpy!
■■■■■■■■■■■■■■■■■■■■■

Jean Claude Jaquettie, with his jacket on.
Jean Claude Jaquettie, with his jacket off.
Jean Claude Jaquettie, with his jacket on.
Jean Claude Jaquettie, with his jacket off.
Jacket on,
Jacket off,
Jacket on,
Jacket off.
Burger burglar. (x3)
■■■■■■■■■■■■■■■■■■■■■

Quick queens quack quick quacks quicker than quacking quails.
■■■■■■■■■■■■■■■■■■■■■

How many wenches could a witch's wench wrench wrench if a witch's wench wrench could wrench wenches. As many wenches as a witch's wench wrench could, if a witch's wench wrench could wrench wenches.
■■■■■■■■■■■■■■■■■■■■■

Washing the washing machine while watching the washing machine washing washing.
■■■■■■■■■■■■■■■■■■■■■

Plaid pleated pants, Plaid pleated pants, Plaid pleated pants, ...
■■■■■■■■■■■■■■■■■■■■■

Drunk drugged ducks, Drunk drugged ducks, Drunk drugged ducks,
■■■■■■■■■■■■■■■■■■■■■

Tongue Twisters

She snapped a selfie with Sophie's silver cell phone.

∎∎∎∎∎∎∎∎∎∎∎∎∎∎∎∎∎∎∎∎∎

She surely suits shiny sleek short skirts.

∎∎∎∎∎∎∎∎∎∎∎∎∎∎∎∎∎∎∎∎∎

Tell Tom the ticket taker to take the ticket to the ticket wicket.

∎∎∎∎∎∎∎∎∎∎∎∎∎∎∎∎∎∎∎∎∎

How many pounds in a groundhog's mound when a groundhog pounds hog mounds?

∎∎∎∎∎∎∎∎∎∎∎∎∎∎∎∎∎∎∎∎∎

Siri said this when asked "How much wood would a woodchuck chuck if a woodchuck could chuck wood? A woodchuck would chuck as much as a woodchuck could chuck, if a woodchuck could chuck wood."

A happy hippo hopped and hiccupped.

∎∎∎∎∎∎∎∎∎∎∎∎∎∎∎∎∎∎∎∎∎

Labradoodle, labradoodle, labradoodle.

∎∎∎∎∎∎∎∎∎∎∎∎∎∎∎∎∎∎∎∎∎

Yelling yellow Yeti.

∎∎∎∎∎∎∎∎∎∎∎∎∎∎∎∎∎∎∎∎∎

Everybody's heard of Peter Piper,
And the peck of pickled peppers that he picked.
That's such a silly simple children's game ,
It hasn't even got a name.
But I'd like to bet that it'll trip you,
And I bet you're gonna have to say you're licked.
If Peter Piper you pronounce with ease.
Then twist your tongue around these.

∎∎∎∎∎∎∎∎∎∎∎∎∎∎∎∎∎∎∎∎∎

Moses supposes his toeses are roses,
But Moses supposes erroneously ,
For Moses he knowses his

toeses aren't roses,
As Moses supposes his toeses to be.
■■■■■■■■■■■■■■■■■■■■■■■

Now Kissle will whistle at busty Miss. Russell
Who'll rustle and bustle till Kissle will roar
So Russell asked Axle for Kissle's dismissal
And this'll teach Kissle to whistle no more.
■■■■■■■■■■■■■■■■■■■■■■■

Tito and Tato were tattooed in total,
But Toto was only tattooed on his toe,
So Tato told Tito where Toto was tattooed,
But Tito said Toto's tattoo wouldn't show.
■■■■■■■■■■■■■■■■■■■■■■■

Theda thought Thora was thumping her thimble,
But Thomas thought Thora was thumping her drum,
Said Theda if Thora's not thumping her thimble,
I think that she surely is thumping her thumb.
■■■■■■■■■■■■■■■■■■■■■■■

Now Charley is chary when choosing his cheeses,
And cheese is a challenge when Charley arrives,
When Charley is charming and chooses a cheddar,
Then chews it and chips it and chops in some chives.
■■■■■■■■■■■■■■■■■■■■■■■

Heda is hoping to hop to Tahiti,
To hack a hibiscus to hang on her hat,
Now Heda has hundreds of hats on her hatrack,
So how can a hop to Tahiti help that.
■■■■■■■■■■■■■■■■■■■■■■■

Snobby Miss. Nora is sniffing her snuffer,
The snuffer's no sniffing it makes Nora sneeze,
When Snyda lets Nort know his Nora is sneezing,

Tongue Twisters

She snappily snorts Nora's sneezing a breeze.

- - -

Sheila is selling her shop at the seashore,
For shops at the seashore are so sure to lose,
And she's not so sure of what she should be selling,
Should Sheila sell seashells or should she sell shoes.

- - -

Colliding, colt riding cowboys, combining colliding while gliding at night coinciding in their fight. It wasn't quite trite even with slight sight, who was right? The fight like light, flashed bright, fast as bears bite flies flying near the bears eyes the fleeing flies die.

- - -

Green and brown blades of grass. (x3)

- - -

Broken blue crayon. (x3)

- - -

Four poor fools filled four pools full.

- - -

Sleep sweetly! Sleep sweetly! Sleep sweetly!

- - -

"The Professor Peter Peckinpah all purpose anti-personnel Peckinpah pocket pistol under the toupee trick" (from the series "Get Smart" (1965) in the episode "Smartucus").

- - -

Purple paper people, purple paper people, purple paper people.

- - -

Shannon shant ship ships through Shilshole.
*(Shilshole is a place in Seattle)

If blue bugs bleed blue blood, and black bugs bleed black blood, do blue-black bugs bleed blue-black blood?

Carolina Herrera resides in the rural area with her running horses.

How many bears could Bear Grills grill if Bear grills could grill bears?

The children eat the chicken in the kitchen.

Cheap Sheep Sheets, Cheap Sheep Sheets, Cheap Sheep Sheets.

It dawned on Don at dawn.

A snake sneaks to seek a snack.

A synonym for cinnamon is a cinnamon synonym.

Great Gate Crasher. (x3)

Sister Susie's sewing shirts for soldiers,
Such saucy soft short shirts for soldiers sister Susie sews,
Some soldiers send epistles say they'd sooner sleep on thistles,
Than those saucy soft short shirts for soldiers,
Sister Susie sews.

How many rats would the ruskies roast if the ruskies could roast rats?
How many cats would a caddie catch if a caddie could catch cats?

Rural ruler. (x3)

Swift shift. (x3)

An illusory vision is a

Tongue Twisters

visionary illusion.

In shoulder surgery some surgeons sew soldiers' shoulders.

Midget minute, midget minute, midget minute.

Willy's wooden whistle wouldn't whistle when Willy went wild.

Wilson Winston winced whilst he minced a squinting prince.

If a dog chews shoes, whose shoes does he choose?

I thought the haughty Professor Tortoise taught ontology, but the naughty Tortoise taught us tautology.

Grandma Gabby Grammer grabbed a gram of gummy goulash. If Grandma Gabby Grammer grabbed a gram of gummy goulash, How many grams of gummy goulash did Grandma Gabby Grammer grab?

"He thrusts his fists against the posts, and still insists he sees the ghosts."

Thrifty Theophilus, the theocratic thistle sifter, thrice thrust three thousand thistles through the slick thick of his softly throbbing thumb.

Hulk Hawk is hulking the hawk, Hawk Hulk is hawking Hulk.
Hawk hugs the hedgehog.

Rather Ruth's writhings than Roth's wrath.
■■■■■■■■■■■■■■■■■■■■■■■■

The third time the three three-toed tree toads tried tying their toes together, the third three-toed tree toad tied the two three-toed tree toads toes to the third toads toes. Then the two tied three-toed tree toads told the third three-toed tree toad that tying their toes together thrilled them to their toe tips.
■■■■■■■■■■■■■■■■■■■■■■■■

Darla's dollars. (x3)
■■■■■■■■■■■■■■■■■■■■■■■■

I see he sees high seas she sees.
■■■■■■■■■■■■■■■■■■■■■■■■

Minsea and Youngsea made this together in their English class
■■■■■■■■■■■■■■■■■■■■■■■■

I saw a kitten eating chicken in the kitchen.
■■■■■■■■■■■■■■■■■■■■■■■■

My back black brake blocks are broken.
■■■■■■■■■■■■■■■■■■■■■■■■

I shot a hippopotamus with bullets made of platinum because if I used leaden ones his hide would surely flatten them.
■■■■■■■■■■■■■■■■■■■■■■■■

Normal word order or inverted word order?
■■■■■■■■■■■■■■■■■■■■■■■■

Peter Rabbit raddish robber. (x3)
■■■■■■■■■■■■■■■■■■■■■■■■

There's a cross on the muzzle of the pistol with the bullet.
But a nick on the handle Of the pistol with the blank.
■■■■■■■■■■■■■■■■■■■■■■■■

"The pellet with the poison's,

Tongue Twisters

In the vessel with the pestle,
The chalice from the palace,
Has the brew that is true."

●●●●●●●●●●●●●●●●●●●●●●●

The Doge did what a Doge does, when a Doge does his duty to a Duke, that is. When the Doge did his duty and the Duke didn't, that's when the Duchess did the dirt to the Duke with the Doge. There they were in the dark: The Duke with his dagger, the Doge with his dart and the Duchess with her dirk. The Duchess dug at the Duke just when the Duke dove at the Doge. Now the Duke ducked, the Doge dodged, and the Duchess didn't. So the Duke got the Duchess, the Duchess got the Doge, and the Doge got the Duke.

●●●●●●●●●●●●●●●●●●●●●●●

Loyal royal lawyer. (x3)

●●●●●●●●●●●●●●●●●●●●●●●

Darn dawn dog gone! (x3)

●●●●●●●●●●●●●●●●●●●●●●●

Free Ritz wristwatch. (x3)

●●●●●●●●●●●●●●●●●●●●●●●

Six slick, slim, slender saplings. (x3)

●●●●●●●●●●●●●●●●●●●●●●●

Tell a tall tale of a tall tailed dog, that told Tim it tap a tall ale and thump the top of Tim's tomb.

●●●●●●●●●●●●●●●●●●●●●●●

Old lady Hunt had a cuzzy Funt not a cuzzy Funt but a Hunt Funt cuzzy.

●●●●●●●●●●●●●●●●●●●●●●●

How much juice does a fruit juice producer produce when a fruit juice producer produces fruit juice? We can deduce a fruit juice produces as much juice as a fruit juice produce can seduce from the fruit that produces

Adam Smith

juice.

They think that their teeth get thinner at times they want to taste thick meat.

Three tired tigers try to throw three trees.

I wish to wish the wish you wish to wish, but if you wish the wish the witch wishes, I won't wish the wish you wish to wish.

Ken can ken that Ken's kin can ken Ken's kin's ken.

Which Swiss witch switched the Swiss wristwatches?

Cook "Cookie" Turk took Kookie Kirk a turkey cookie.

How many tow trucks could a tow truck tow if a tow truck could tow tow trucks.

I miss my Swiss miss.
My Swiss miss misses me.

Now the trees are all groaning in growling, rough gales.
That with thuds and hoarse roaring roll raging around!
Such leaf-rousing, branch-ruining, ripping, raw wails,
Such a terrible, thrashing and tree-wrecking sound!

Slinking, sliding, slithering slyly,
Swiftly slipping through the grasses shyly,
Silent but for swish and hiss
Is the sinuous snake's leglessness.

Corythosaurus bit the gory

Tongue Twisters

esophagus of the dillapitated Dilophosaurus who lived in the sorest of forests with the whacky pachy-rinosaurus and the ceratosaurus, but the most poorest and mourish panoplosaurus called Wang sang and rang chorus with the lurdusaurus and the brachiosaurus who was dying of staphylococus-aureas.
••••••••••••••••••••••••

How much squash could a sasquatch squish, if a sasquatch could squish squash?
••••••••••••••••••••••••

Fresh fish and fried prawns. (x3)
••••••••••••••••••••••••

She thrust three thousand thistles through the thick of her thumb.
••••••••••••••••••••••••

Who washed Washington's white woolen underwear when Washington's washerwoman went west?
••••••••••••••••••••••••

On mules we find two legs behind and two we find before.
We stand behind before we find what those behind be for.
••••••••••••••••••••••••

Three grey geese
In a green field grazing,
Grey were the geese.
And green was the grazing.
••••••••••••••••••••••••

Susie sits shinning silver shoes
••••••••••••••••••••••••

Ralph rakes leaves really, really lousily. (x3)
••••••••••••••••••••••••

Lady Luck dislikes losers. (x3)
••••••••••••••••••••••••

Broken back brake block.
(x3)
■■■■■■■■■■■■■■■■■■■■■■

Mumbling, bumbling. Bumbling, mumbling. (x3)
■■■■■■■■■■■■■■■■■■■■■■

Of all the felt I ever felt I never felt felt that felt like that felt felt.
■■■■■■■■■■■■■■■■■■■■■■

They hatch fish at the state fish hatchery and sell hatched fish to the fish stick factory.

In pine tar is. In oak none is. In mud eels are. In clay none is.
■■■■■■■■■■■■■■■■■■■■■■

The sixth sick sheik's sixth sick sheep.
■■■■■■■■■■■■■■■■■■■■■■

Thirty-six thick silk threads.
■■■■■■■■■■■■■■■■■■■■■■

Silly shoe-fly pie fans sell chilly shoe-fly pie pans.
■■■■■■■■■■■■■■■■■■■■■■

Kantai can tie a tie. If Kantai can tie a tie,
why can't I tie a tie like Kantai can tie a tie.
■■■■■■■■■■■■■■■■■■■■■■

The two-toed tree toad tried to tread where the three-toed tree toad trod.
■■■■■■■■■■■■■■■■■■■■■■

Tricky Tristan tracked a trail of tiny turtles.
How many tiny turtles did Tricky Tristan track?
Tricky Tristan tracked twenty two tiny turtles;
That's how many tiny turtles tricky Tristan tracked.

Esau Wood saw a wood saw, saw wood, as no wood saw would saw wood. If Esau Wood saw a wood saw, saw wood, as no wood saw would saw wood, where is the wood saw witch would saw wood, as no wood saw

Tongue Twisters

would saw wood.

You're behaving like a babbling, bumbling band of baboons.

Iranian Uranium. (x3)

Giddy kiddy goat,
Giddy kiddy goat,
Giddy, giddy, giddy, giddy, giddy, kiddy goat.

He wanted to desert his dessert in the desert! (x3)

If a Hottentot tot taught a Hottentot tot to talk before the tot would totter, ought the Hottentot tot be taught to say ought, or naught, or what ought to be taught the Hottentot tot? If to hoot and to toot a Hottentot tot be taught by a Hottentot tutor, should the tutor get hot if the Hottentot tot hoots and toots at the Hottentot tutor?

There was a writer called Wright, he taught his son to write Wright right:
"It's not right to write Wright 'Rite', please try to write Wright right!"

Very rare vagrant wader. (x3)

Crash Quiche Course. (x3)

I broke a brickbat and a brickbat broke me. (x3)

A wooden worm wouldn't be worthy of worship but would he if he wondered and worried about what he would be worthy of if he wasn't wooden?

Give papa a cup of proper coffee in a copper

coffee cup.

Nine nice night nurses nursing nicely. (x3)

Farrell's features fabulous food 'n' fantastic fountain fantasies for frolicking, fun-filled festive families.

Who holds Joe's nose when he blows? Joe knows.

Thirty-three thousand feathers on a thrushes throat.

When I went to Warsaw, I saw a saw that could outsaw any saw that I ever saw. Now, if you go to Warsaw and see a saw that could outsaw the saw I saw, I'd like to see your saw saw.

If practice makes perfect and perfect needs practice, I'm perfectly practiced and practically perfect.

Six Czech cricket critics. (x3)

Rubber Berber Gerber Burger. (x3)

Lucid Lou slued loose the sluice that slew the slough.

In Hertford, Hereford and Hampshire hurricanes hardly ever happen.

Thomas Tattamus took two T's to tie two tots to two tall trees.

Hercules, a hardy hunter, hunted a hare in the Hampshire Hills. Hit him on

Tongue Twisters

the head with a hard, hard hammer and he howled horribly!

Frank's fisher fishes on Friday for Frank's Friday fresh fried fish-fest.

I saw a saw in Warsaw. Of all the saws I ever saw I never saw a saw that could saw, like the saw I saw in Warsaw.

Dina had a dog,
the dog dug,
the dog dug deep,
how deep did Dina's dog dig?
Dina had a duck,
the duck dived,
the duck dived deep,
how deep did Dina's duck dive?
Dina's duck dived as deep as Dina's dog dug!

It's a nice night for a white rice fight. (x3)

If a fella met a fella in a field of fitches,
Can a fella tell a fella where a fella itches?

I feel a feel a funny feel a funny feel feel I, If I feel a funny feel a funny feel feel I.

Never trust
a sloppy crust,
a squally gust,
ships that rust,
or girls with lust.
But if you must,
you may trust
to go bust,
and back to dust,
which serves you just.

This is a story about four people named Everybody, Somebody, Anybody and Nobody. There was an important job to be done and Everybody was sure that Somebody would do it. Anybody could have done it, but Nobody did it. Somebody got angry about that, because it was Everybody's job. Everybody thought Anybody could do it, but Nobody realised that Everybody wouldn't do it. It ended up that Everybody blamed Somebody, when Nobody did, what Anybody could have done.

Mr. Knott and Mr. Watt on the Phone

-Hello?
-Who's calling?
-Watt.
-What's your name?
-Watt's my name.
-Yes, what is your name?
-My name is John Watt.
-John what?
-Yes.
-...I'll call on you this afternoon.
-All right, are you Jones?
-No, I'm Knott.
-Will you tell me your name, then?
-Will Knott.
-Why not?
-My name is Knott.
-Not what?
-Not Watt. Knott.
-What?

Round brown bread. (x3)

Grip glue, grip glue, grip glue.

Bob's pop-up blocker blocks Bob's pop-ups. (x3)

Chill, Shake, Serve. (x3)

M. R. Ducks,
M.R. not Ducks,
O. S. M. R.,
L. I'll B.,
M. R. Ducks!

A cunning young canner from Canning,

Tongue Twisters

Once observed to his granny,
"A canner can can a lot of things gran,
But a canner can't can a can, can he?"
■■■■■■■■■■■■■■■■■■■■■

How many ducks could a duck duct-tape, if a duck could duct-tape ducks?
■■■■■■■■■■■■■■■■■■■■■

Bad dead bed-bugs bleed bug blood. (x3)
■■■■■■■■■■■■■■■■■■■■■

Upper roller, lower roller, upper roller, lower roller, upper roller, lower roller.
■■■■■■■■■■■■■■■■■■■■■

Bill had a billboard, Bill also had a board bill. The billboard bored Bill so Bill sold the billboard to pay for the board bill.
■■■■■■■■■■■■■■■■■■■■■

Faith's face cloth, Faith's face cloth, Faith's face cloth.
■■■■■■■■■■■■■■■■■■■■■

Deer, deer, oh dear, oh dear, your career as a deer is over here no, no, oh no, although your career as a skellytun's begun.
■■■■■■■■■■■■■■■■■■■■■

Click, clap, pluck. (x3)
■■■■■■■■■■■■■■■■■■■■■

Mister Twister's tongue twisters. (x3)
■■■■■■■■■■■■■■■■■■■■■

Hum-min-a, Hum-min-a, Hum-min-a.
■■■■■■■■■■■■■■■■■■■■■

Mud bug, mud bug, mud bug.
■■■■■■■■■■■■■■■■■■■■■

Polish it in the corner.
Polish it in the corner.
Polish it in the corner.
■■■■■■■■■■■■■■■■■■■■■

I gratefully gazed at the gracefully grazing gazelles.
■■■■■■■■■■■■■■■■■■■■■

Adam Smith

Really very weary, really very weary, really very weary.

Six sticky skeletons,
six sticky skeletons,
six sticky skeletons.

■■■■■■■■■■■■■■■■■■■■■■■■

Sheila is selling her shop at the seashore,
For shops at the seashore are so sure to lose,
And she's not so sure of what she should be selling
Should Sheila sell seashells or should she sell shoes.

■■■■■■■■■■■■■■■■■■■■■■■■

A canner exceedingly canny,
One morning remarked to his granny,
A canner can can,
Anything that he can,
But a canner can't can a can; can he?

■■■■■■■■■■■■■■■■■■■■■■■■

She sat upon a balcony, inimicably mimicking him hiccuping and amicably welcoming him in.

■■■■■■■■■■■■■■■■■■■■■■■■

I can't believe that "I Can't Believe It's Not Butter!" is actually a butter that I can't believe is not butter.

■■■■■■■■■■■■■■■■■■■■■■■■

You name it, we claim it. If we can't get it, we'll send you to get it. If we can't send you to get it, forgit it. Who's got it, if we don't got it?

■■■■■■■■■■■■■■■■■■■■■■■■

If your Bob doesnt give our Bob that bob that your Bob owes our Bob, our Bob will give your Bob a bob in the eye.

■■■■■■■■■■■■■■■■■■■■■■■■

V: Voilà! In view, a humble vaudevillian veteran, cast vicariously as both victim and villain by the vicissitudes of Fate. This visage, no mere veneer of

Tongue Twisters

vanity, is a vestige of the vox populi, now vacant, vanished. However, this valorous visitation of a bygone vexation, stands vivified and has vowed to vanquish these venal and virulent vermin vanguarding vice and vouchsafing the violently vicious and voracious violation of volition.
[carves V into poster on wall]
V: The only verdict is vengeance; a vendetta, held as a votive, not in vain, for the value and veracity of such shall one day vindicate the vigilant and the virtuous.
[giggles]
V: Verily, this vichyssoise of verbiage veers most verbose, so let me simply add that it's my very good honor to meet you and you may call me V.
*(from the screenplay of the movie "V for Vendetta", at the beginning, when V meets Evie for the first time)

∎∎∎∎∎∎∎∎∎∎∎∎∎∎∎∎∎∎∎∎∎∎∎

Chip shop chips. (x3)
∎∎∎∎∎∎∎∎∎∎∎∎∎∎∎∎∎∎∎∎∎∎∎

Velvet Revolver,
Velvet Revolver,
Velvet Revolver.
∎∎∎∎∎∎∎∎∎∎∎∎∎∎∎∎∎∎∎∎∎∎∎

Shine my city shoes. (x3)
∎∎∎∎∎∎∎∎∎∎∎∎∎∎∎∎∎∎∎∎∎∎∎

Sniff Sesh! Sniff Sesh! Sniff Sesh!
∎∎∎∎∎∎∎∎∎∎∎∎∎∎∎∎∎∎∎∎∎∎∎

The Knight said, "He's", with niceties, "some nights a tease or nice at ease on nice settees".
∎∎∎∎∎∎∎∎∎∎∎∎∎∎∎∎∎∎∎∎∎∎∎

How much snus could a moose on the loose use
if a moose on the loose could use loose snus?
∎∎∎∎∎∎∎∎∎∎∎∎∎∎∎∎∎∎∎∎∎∎∎

Black Rock Brain Lock. (x3)
∎∎∎∎∎∎∎∎∎∎∎∎∎∎∎∎∎∎∎∎∎∎∎

Which Witch snitched the Snitch Witch?
Or did the Snitch Witch snitch the Witch?
If the Snitch Witch snitched the Witch then which Witch did the Snitch Witch snitch?
■■■■■■■■■■■■■■■■■■■■■■■

A maid named Lady Marmalade made mainly lard and lemonade.
M'lady lamely never made a well-named, labelled marmalade.
■■■■■■■■■■■■■■■■■■■■■■■

Theodore Thistle threw three thorny thistles.
How many thorny thistles did Theodore Thistle throw?
■■■■■■■■■■■■■■■■■■■■■■■

Silly Sally Shouldnort shaved sheep she should show soon so selling sheep shaved showed she shouldn't show shaved sheep so soon.
■■■■■■■■■■■■■■■■■■■■■■■

Cracker rapper,
cracker rapper,
cracker rapper.
■■■■■■■■■■■■■■■■■■■■■■■

Lenny Lou leopard led leprechauns leaping like lemmings.
■■■■■■■■■■■■■■■■■■■■■■■

No need to light a nightlight on a light night like tonight.
■■■■■■■■■■■■■■■■■■■■■■■

I wish to wish, I dream to dream, I try to try, and I live to live, and I'd die to die, and I cry to cry but I dont know why.
■■■■■■■■■■■■■■■■■■■■■■■

My mommy makes me muffins on Mondays.
■■■■■■■■■■■■■■■■■■■■■■■

A real rare whale. (x3)
■■■■■■■■■■■■■■■■■■■■■■■

Tongue Twisters

Terry Teeter, a teeter-totter teacher, taught her daughter Tara to teeter-totter, but Tara Teeter didn't teeter-totter as Terry Teeter taught her to.

Ken Dodd's dad's dog 's dead.

▪▪▪▪▪▪▪▪▪▪▪▪▪▪▪▪▪▪▪▪▪▪▪

I bought a bit of baking powder and baked a batch of biscuits. I brought a big basket of biscuits back to the bakery and baked a basket of big biscuits. Then I took the big basket of biscuits and the basket of big biscuits and mixed the big biscuits with the basket of biscuits that was next to the big basket and put a bunch of biscuits from the basket into a biscuit mixer and brought the basket of biscuits and the box of mixed biscuits and the biscuit mixer to the bakery and opened a tin of sardines.

*(Said to be a diction test for would-be radio announcers: To be read clearly, without mistakes, in less than 20 seconds).

▪▪▪▪▪▪▪▪▪▪▪▪▪▪▪▪▪▪▪▪▪▪▪

Karla is a masai girl. She can tie a tie and untie a tie. If Karla can tie a tie and untie a tie, why can't I tie a tie and untie a tie?

▪▪▪▪▪▪▪▪▪▪▪▪▪▪▪▪▪▪▪▪▪▪▪

I'm a mother pheasant plucker,
I pluck mother pheasants.
I'm the most pleasant mother pheasant plucker,
to ever pluck a mother pheasant. Actually, ...
I'm Not the pheasant plucker,
I'm the pheasant plucker's son.
But I'll stay and pluck the pheasants
Till the pheasant plucking 's done!

▪▪▪▪▪▪▪▪▪▪▪▪▪▪▪▪▪▪▪▪▪▪▪

If you go for a gopher a

gopher will go for a gopher hole.

Seven slick and sexy sealskin ski suits slid slowly down the slope.

The chief of the Leith police dismisseth us.

Fred Threlfall's thirty-five fine threads are finer threads than Fred Threlfall's thirty-five thick threads.

Bug's black blood, Black bug's blood. (x3)

Reed Wade Road. (x3)

Jack's nap sack strap snapped.

I saw Esau sitting on a seesaw. I saw Esau; he saw me.

A quick witted cricket critic.

Hitchcock Hawk Watch Spots Record Raptors.

Sure, sir, the ship's sure shipshape, sir.

The Smothers brothers' father's mother's brothers are the Smothers brothers' mother's father's other brothers.

One Double Dozen Double Damask Dinner Napkins.

The cat crept into the crypt, crapped and crept out.

Tongue Twisters

Dear mother,
give your other udder,
to my other brother.

••••••••••••••••••••••••

Furnish Freddie's nursery with forty-four furry Furby Beanie Babies.

••••••••••••••••••••••••

Arnold Palmer,
Arnold Palmer,
Arnold Palmer.

••••••••••••••••••••••••

A bitter biting bittern bit a better biting bittern,
And the better biting bittern bit the bitter biting bittern back.
Said the bitter biting bittern to the better biting bittern,
"I'm a bitter biting bittern bitten back".

••••••••••••••••••••••••

Certified certificates from certified certificate certifiers.

••••••••••••••••••••••••

Imagine, imagining imagining, an imaginary imaginary imaginary menagerie manager, imagining imagining imagining an imaginary imaginary imaginary managerie.
What noise annoys a noisy oyster?
Any noise annoys a noisy oyster,
but a noisy noise annoys a noisy oyster most!

••••••••••••••••••••••••

We need a plan to fan a pan; find a pan to fan, then find a fan to fan the pan, then fan the pan.

••••••••••••••••••••••••

How many snacks could a snack stacker stack, if a snack stacker snacked stacked snacks?

••••••••••••••••••••••••

Freddy is ready to roast red roaches.
Ready for Freddy's roasted

red roaches?

••••••••••••••••••••••

I thought a thought.

But the thought I thought Wasn't the thought I thought I thought.

If the thought I thought I thought,

Had been the thought I thought,

I wouldn't have thought I thought.

••••••••••••••••••••••

She sells sea shells on the seashore.

The seashells she sells are seashells she is sure.

••••••••••••••••••••••

A noise annoys an oyster, but a noisy noise annoys an oyster more!

••••••••••••••••••••••

Plain bun, plum bun, bun without plum.

••••••••••••••••••••••

Slick slim slippers sliding south.

••••••••••••••••••••••

The Leith police dismisseth us,

They thought we sought to stay;

The Leith police dismisseth us,

They thought we'd stay all day.

The Leith police dismisseth us,

We both sighed sighs apiece;

And the sighs that we sighed as we said goodbye,

Were the size of the Leith police.

••••••••••••••••••••••

Ah shucks, six stick shifts stuck shut!

••••••••••••••••••••••

Meter maid Mary married manly Matthew Marcus Mayo,

a moody male mailman moving mostly metered mail.

••••••••••••••••••••••

Tongue Twisters

The king would sing, about a ring that would go ding.
••••••••••••••••••••••••

How much dough would Bob Dole dole if Bob Dole could dole dough?
Bob Dole would dole as much dough as Bob Dole could dole, if Bob Dole could dole dough.

People pledging plenty of pennies.
••••••••••••••••••••••••

Mares eat oats and does eat oats, but little lambs eat ivy.
••••••••••••••••••••••••

To begin to toboggan,
first buy a toboggan.
But don't buy too big a toboggan.
Too big a toboggan is too big a toboggan to buy to begin to toboggan.
••••••••••••••••••••••••

Switch watch, wrist watch.
••••••••••••••••••••••••

Sinful Caesar sipped his snifter, seized his knees and sneezed.
••••••••••••••••••••••••

Chester chooses chestnuts, cheddar cheese with chewy chives.
He chews them and he chooses them.
He chooses them and he chews them
Those chestnuts, cheddar cheese
and chives in cheery, charming chunks.
••••••••••••••••••••••••

Moses supposes his toeses are roses.
But Moses supposes erroneously.
Moses, he knowses his toeses aren't roses
As Moses supposes his toeses to be.
••••••••••••••••••••••••

I wish I were what I was

when I wished I were what I am.

∎∎∎∎∎∎∎∎∎∎∎∎∎∎∎∎∎∎∎∎∎∎∎

She sells seashells on the seashore. The seashells she sells are seashore seashells.

∎∎∎∎∎∎∎∎∎∎∎∎∎∎∎∎∎∎∎∎∎∎∎

Irish wristwatch. (x3)

∎∎∎∎∎∎∎∎∎∎∎∎∎∎∎∎∎∎∎∎∎∎∎

She had shoulder surgery.
(x3)

∎∎∎∎∎∎∎∎∎∎∎∎∎∎∎∎∎∎∎∎∎∎∎

To put a pipe in byte mode, type PIPE_TYPE_BYTE.

∎∎∎∎∎∎∎∎∎∎∎∎∎∎∎∎∎∎∎∎∎∎∎

Three tree turtles took turns talking tongue twisters.
If three tree turtles took turns talking tongue twisters,
where's the twisters the three tree turtles talked?

∎∎∎∎∎∎∎∎∎∎∎∎∎∎∎∎∎∎∎∎∎∎∎

Oh, the sadness of her sadness when she's sad.
Oh, the gladness of her gladness when she's glad.
But the sadness of her sadness,
and the gladness of her gladness,
Are nothing like her madness when she's mad!

∎∎∎∎∎∎∎∎∎∎∎∎∎∎∎∎∎∎∎∎∎∎∎

I would if I could, and if I couldn't, how could I?
You couldn't, unless you could, could you?

∎∎∎∎∎∎∎∎∎∎∎∎∎∎∎∎∎∎∎∎∎∎∎

Give me the gift of a grip-top sock,
A clip drape shipshape tip top sock.
Not your spinslick slapstick slipshod stock,
But a plastic, elastic grip-top sock.
None of your fantastic slack swap slop
From a slap dash flash cash haberdash shop.
Not a knick knack knitlock knockneed knickerbocker

Tongue Twisters

sock
With a mock-shot blob-mottled trick-ticker top clock.
Not a supersheet seersucker rucksack sock,
Not a spot-speckled frog-freckled cheap sheik's sock
Off a hodge-podge moss-blotched scotch-botched block.
Nothing slipshod drip drop flip flop or glip glop
Tip me to a tip top grip top sock.
*(articulation warmup for actors).
■■■■■■■■■■■■■■■■■■■■■■■

National Sheepshire Sheep Association. (x3)
■■■■■■■■■■■■■■■■■■■■■■■

The crow flew over the river with a lump of raw liver.
■■■■■■■■■■■■■■■■■■■■■■■

The little red lorry went down Limuru road.

*(Limuru (Lee-moo-roo) road is a the name of a road in Kenya.)
■■■■■■■■■■■■■■■■■■■■■■■

Flies fly but a fly flies. (x3)
■■■■■■■■■■■■■■■■■■■■■■■

Did Doug dig Dick's garden or did Dick dig Doug's garden?
■■■■■■■■■■■■■■■■■■■■■■■

If a Hottentot taught a Hottentot tot to talk ere the tot could totter, ought the Hottentot tot be taught to say ought or naught or what ought to be taught 'er?
■■■■■■■■■■■■■■■■■■■■■■■

How many cans can a canner can if a canner can can cans? A canner can can as many cans as a canner can if a canner can can cans.
■■■■■■■■■■■■■■■■■■■■■■■

Federal Express is now called FedEx.

When I retire I'll be a FedEx ex.
But if I'm an officer when I retire, I'll be an ex Fedex Exec.
Then after a divorce, my ex-wife will be an ex FedEx exec's ex.
If I rejoin FedEx in time, I'd be an ex ex FedEx exec.
When we remarry, my wife will be an ex ex FedEx exec's ex.

• •

Which witch snitched the stitched switch for which the Swiss witch wished?

• •

Does this shop sport short socks with spots?

• •

Customer: Do you have soothers?
Shopkeeper (thinking he had said "scissors"): No, we don't have scissors.
Customer: Soothers!
Shopkeeper : No, we don't have scissors or soothers.
... scissors or soothers, scissors or soothers, scissors or soothers, ...

• •

Tommy, Tommy, toiling in a tailor's shop.
All day long he fits and tucks,
all day long he tucks and fits,
and fits and tucks, and tucks and fits,
and fits and tucks, and tucks and fits.
Tommy, Tommy, toiling in a tailor's shop.

• •

A flea and a fly in a flue, were imprisoned. So what could they do?
Said the fly, "Let us flee".
Said the flea, "Let us fly".
So they flew through a flaw in the flue.

• •

King Thistle stuck a thousand thistles in the thistle of his thumb.

Tongue Twisters

A thousand thistles King Thistle stuck in the thistle of his thumb.
If King Thistle stuck a thousand thistles in the thistle of his thumb,
How many thistles did King Thistle stick in the thistle of his thumb?

∎∎∎∎∎∎∎∎∎∎∎∎∎∎∎∎∎∎∎∎∎∎

Five fat friars frying flat fish. (x3)

∎∎∎∎∎∎∎∎∎∎∎∎∎∎∎∎∎∎∎∎∎∎

The bottle of perfume that Willy sent
was highly displeasing to Millicent.
Her thanks were so cold that they quarreled, I'm told
o'er that silly scent Willy sent Millicent

∎∎∎∎∎∎∎∎∎∎∎∎∎∎∎∎∎∎∎∎∎∎

Esau Wood sawed wood. All the wood Esau Wood saw, Esau Wood would saw. All the wood Wood saw, Esau sought to saw. One day Esau Wood's wood-saw would saw no wood. So Esau Wood sought a new wood-saw. The new wood-saw would saw wood. Oh, the wood Esau Wood would saw. Esau sought a saw that would saw wood as no other wood-saw would saw. And Esau found a saw that would saw as no other wood-saw would saw. And Esau Wood sawed wood.

∎∎∎∎∎∎∎∎∎∎∎∎∎∎∎∎∎∎∎∎∎∎

A skunk sat on a stump and thunk the stump stunk, but the stump thunk the skunk stunk.

∎∎∎∎∎∎∎∎∎∎∎∎∎∎∎∎∎∎∎∎∎∎

Extinct insects' instincts, extant insects' instincts.

∎∎∎∎∎∎∎∎∎∎∎∎∎∎∎∎∎∎∎∎∎∎

Sweater weather, leather weather. (x3)

∎∎∎∎∎∎∎∎∎∎∎∎∎∎∎∎∎∎∎∎∎∎

One black beetle bled

only black blood, the other black beetle bled blue.

The big black bug's blood ran blue.

I am not the pheasant plucker,
I'm the pheasant plucker's mate.
I am only plucking pheasants
'cause the pheasant plucker's late.

Ed Nott was shot and Sam Shott was not. So it is better to be Shott than Nott. Some say Nott was not shot. But Shott says he shot Nott. Either the shot Shott shot at Nott was not shot, or Nott was shot. If the shot Shott shot shot Nott, Nott was shot. But if the shot Shott shot shot Shott, the shot was Shott, not Nott. However, the shot Shott shot shot not Shott - but Nott. So, Ed Nott was shot and that's hot! Is it not?

We will learn why her lowly lone, worn yarn loom will rarely earn immoral money.

Unique New York,
unique New York,
unique New York.

If Dr. Seuss Were a Technical Writer.....

Here's an easy game to play.
Here's an easy thing to say:

If a packet hits a pocket on a socket on a port,
And the bus is interrupted as a very last resort,
And the address of the memory makes your floppy disk abort,

Tongue Twisters

Then the socket packet pocket has an error to report!

If your cursor finds a menu item followed by a dash,
And the double-clicking icon puts your window in the trash,
And your data is corrupted 'cause the index doesn't hash,
then your situation's hopeless, and your system's gonna crash!

You can't say this? What a shame, sir!
We'll find you another game, sir.

If the label on the cable on the table at your house,
Says the network is connected to the button on your mouse,
But your packets want to tunnel on another protocol,
That's repeatedly rejected by the printer down the hall,
And your screen is all distorted by the side effects of gauss,
So your icons in the window are as wavy as a souse,
Then you may as well reboot and go out with a bang,
'Cause as sure as I'm a poet, the sucker's gonna hang!

When the copy of your floppy's getting sloppy on the disk,
And the microcode instructions cause unnecessary risk,
Then you have to flash your memory and you'll want to ram your rom.
Quickly turn off the computer and be sure to tell your mom!

■■■■■■■■■■■■■■■■■■■■■■■■■

Picky people pick Peter

Pan Peanut Butter.
Peter Pan Peanut is the peanut picky people pick.

Ray Rag ran across a rough road.
Across a rough road Ray Rag ran.
Where is the rough road Ray Rag ran across?

A Tudor who tooted the flute
tried to tutor two tooters to toot.
Said the two to the tutor,
"Is it harder to toot or
to tutor two tooters to toot?"

Mrs. Puggy Wuggy has a square cut punt.
Not a punt cut square,
Just a square cut punt.
It's round in the stern and blunt in the front.
Mrs Puggy Wuggy has a square cut punt.

Tim, the thin twin tinsmith. (x3)

Thin sticks, thick bricks. (x3)

Red lorry, yellow lorry. (x3)

A big black bug bit a big black bear and made the big black bear bleed blood.

How much wood would a woodchuck chuck if a woodchuck would chuck wood? A woodchuck would chuck how much a woodchuck would chuck if a woodchuck would chuck wood.

Larry Hurley, a burly squirrel hurler, hurled a furry squirrel through a curly grill.

Tongue Twisters

Six twin screwed steel steam cruisers.

A nurse anesthetist unearthed a nest.

Blake's black bike's back brake bracket block broke.

Each Easter Eddie eats eighty Easter eggs.

She slits the sheet she sits on.

A rough-coated, dough-faced, thoughtful ploughman strode through the streets of Scarborough; after falling into a slough, he coughed and hiccoughed.
A twister of twists once twisted a twist.
And the twist that he twisted was a three-twisted twist.
Now in twisting this twist, if a twist should untwist, would the twist that untwisted untwist the twists?

Red lolly, yellow lolly.

Mrs. Hunt had a country cut front in the front of her country cut pettycoat.

Knapsack strap.

Miss Smith's fish-sauce shop seldom sells shellfish.

Great gray goats. (x3)

Whether the weather be fine or whether the weather be not.
Whether the weather be cold or whether the weather be hot.
We'll weather the weather

whether we like it or not.
••••••••••••••••••••••••

Sunshine city,
sunshine city,
sunshine city.
••••••••••••••••••••••••

The batter with the butter is the batter that is better!
••••••••••••••••••••••••

There's a sandwich on the sand which was sent by a sane witch.
••••••••••••••••••••••••

How many yaks could a yak pack pack if a yak pack could pack yaks?
••••••••••••••••••••••••

Twelve twins twirled twelve twigs.
••••••••••••••••••••••••

If you stick a stock of liquor in your locker it is slick to stick a lock upon your stock or some joker who is slicker is going to trick you of your liquor if you fail to lock your liquor with a lock.
••••••••••••••••••••••••

Clowns grow glowing crowns.
••••••••••••••••••••••••

Can you imagine an imaginary menagerie manager imagining managing an imaginary menagerie?
••••••••••••••••••••••••

Sister Suzie sewing shirts for soldiers,
Such skill as sewing shirts,
Our shy young sister Suzie shows,
Some soldiers send epistles,
Say they'd rather sleep in thistles,
Than the saucy, soft short shirts for soldiers Sister Suzie sews.

Red leather, yellow leather.
••••••••••••••••••••••••

Two to two to Tooting

Tongue Twisters

too!

∎∎∎∎∎∎∎∎∎∎∎∎∎∎∎∎∎∎∎∎∎∎∎∎

Richard's wretched ratchet wrench.

∎∎∎∎∎∎∎∎∎∎∎∎∎∎∎∎∎∎∎∎∎∎∎∎

Rugged rubber baby buggy bumpers.

∎∎∎∎∎∎∎∎∎∎∎∎∎∎∎∎∎∎∎∎∎∎∎∎

A box of biscuits, a box of mixed biscuits, and a biscuit mixer.

∎∎∎∎∎∎∎∎∎∎∎∎∎∎∎∎∎∎∎∎∎∎∎∎

When a doctor doctors a doctor, does the doctor doing the doctoring doctor as the doctor being doctored wants to be doctored or does the doctor doing the doctoring doctor as he wants to doctor?

∎∎∎∎∎∎∎∎∎∎∎∎∎∎∎∎∎∎∎∎∎∎∎∎

What to do to die today at a minute or two to two. A terribly difficult thing to say and a harder thing to do. A dragon will come and beat his drum Ra-ta-ta-ta-ta-ta-ta-ta-too at a minute or two to two today. At a minute or two to two.

∎∎∎∎∎∎∎∎∎∎∎∎∎∎∎∎∎∎∎∎∎∎∎∎

If two witches would watch two watches, which witch would watch which watch?

∎∎∎∎∎∎∎∎∎∎∎∎∎∎∎∎∎∎∎∎∎∎∎∎

The soldier's shoulder surely hurts!

∎∎∎∎∎∎∎∎∎∎∎∎∎∎∎∎∎∎∎∎∎∎∎∎

She sees seas slapping shores.

∎∎∎∎∎∎∎∎∎∎∎∎∎∎∎∎∎∎∎∎∎∎∎∎

A loyal warrior will rarely worry why we rule.

∎∎∎∎∎∎∎∎∎∎∎∎∎∎∎∎∎∎∎∎∎∎∎∎

Greek grapes. (x3)

∎∎∎∎∎∎∎∎∎∎∎∎∎∎∎∎∎∎∎∎∎∎∎∎

Mr. See owned a saw and Mr Soar owned a seesaw. Now See's saw sawed

Soar's seesaw before Soar saw See.

••••••••••••••••••••••••

Six sick sea-serpents swam the seven seas.

••••••••••••••••••••••••

There was a little witch which switched from Chichester to Ipswich.

••••••••••••••••••••••••

••••••••••••••••••••••••

A proper cup of coffee from a proper copper coffee pot.

••••••••••••••••••••••••

Don't trouble trouble, until trouble troubles you! If you trouble trouble, triple trouble troubles you!

••••••••••••••••••••••••

Theophilus Thadeus Thistledown, the succesful thistle-sifter, while sifting a sieve-full of unsifted thistles, thrust three thousand thistles through the thick of his thumb. Now, if Theophilus Thadeus Thistledown, the succesful thistle-sifter, thrust three thousand thistles through the thick of his thumb, see that thou, while sifting a sieve-full of unsifted thistles, thrust not three thousand thistles through the thick of thy thumb.

••••••••••••••••••••••••

Shoe section,
shoe section,
shoe section.

••••••••••••••••••••••••

A smart fella, a fella smart.
It takes a smart fella to say a fella smart.

••••••••••••••••••••••••

She is a thistle-sifter. She has a sieve of unsifted thistles and a sieve of sifted thistles and the sieve of unsifted thistles she sifts into the sieve of sifted thistles because she is a thistle-sifter.

••••••••••••••••••••••••

Tongue Twisters

Admidst the mists and coldest frosts,
With stoutest wrists and loudest boasts,
He thrusts his fists against the posts,
And still insists he sees the ghosts.
■■■■■■■■■■■■■■■■■■■■■■

Fuzzy Wuzzy was a bear,
Fuzzy Wuzzy had no hair,
Fuzzy Wuzzy wasn't very fuzzy, was he?
■■■■■■■■■■■■■■■■■■■■■■

Blue glue gun, green glue gun. (x3)
■■■■■■■■■■■■■■■■■■■■■■

Mallory's hourly salary. (x3)
■■■■■■■■■■■■■■■■■■■■■■

I slit a sheet, a sheet I slit, and on that slitted sheet I sit.

Don't spring on the inner-spring this spring or there will be an offspring next spring.
■■■■■■■■■■■■■■■■■■■■■■

Bake big batches of bitter brown bread. (x3)
■■■■■■■■■■■■■■■■■■■■■■

But she as far surpasseth Sycorax,
As great'st does least.
*(Caliban describing Miranda's beauty in 'The Tempest", by William Shakespeare).
■■■■■■■■■■■■■■■■■■■■■■

Bake big batches of brown blueberry bread.
■■■■■■■■■■■■■■■■■■■■■■

She sits in her slip and sips Schlitz.
■■■■■■■■■■■■■■■■■■■■■■

Which wristwatch is a Swiss wristwatch?
■■■■■■■■■■■■■■■■■■■■■■

Whoever slit the sheets is a good sheet slitter.
Mummies make money. (x3)
■■■■■■■■■■■■■■■■■■■■■■

Crush grapes,
grapes crush,
crush grapes.
■■■■■■■■■■■■■■■■■■■■■■

Adam Smith

An elephant was asphyxiated in the asphalt.
▪▪▪▪▪▪▪▪▪▪▪▪▪▪▪▪▪▪▪▪▪▪▪▪

A black bloke's back brake-block broke.
▪▪▪▪▪▪▪▪▪▪▪▪▪▪▪▪▪▪▪▪▪▪▪▪

This is a zither. (x3)
▪▪▪▪▪▪▪▪▪▪▪▪▪▪▪▪▪▪▪▪▪▪▪▪

Fresh fried fish,
Fish fresh fried,
Fried fish fresh,
Fish fried fresh.
▪▪▪▪▪▪▪▪▪▪▪▪▪▪▪▪▪▪▪▪▪▪▪▪

There was a minimum of cinnamon in the aluminum pan.
▪▪▪▪▪▪▪▪▪▪▪▪▪▪▪▪▪▪▪▪▪▪▪▪

Really leery, rarely Larry.
▪▪▪▪▪▪▪▪▪▪▪▪▪▪▪▪▪▪▪▪▪▪▪▪

Big black bugs bleed blue black blood but baby black bugs bleed blue blood.
▪▪▪▪▪▪▪▪▪▪▪▪▪▪▪▪▪▪▪▪▪▪▪▪

Elizabeth has eleven elves in her elm tree.
▪▪▪▪▪▪▪▪▪▪▪▪▪▪▪▪▪▪▪▪▪▪▪▪

Her whole right hand really hurts.
*(difficult in Brazil).
▪▪▪▪▪▪▪▪▪▪▪▪▪▪▪▪▪▪▪▪▪▪▪▪

Come, come,
Stay calm, stay calm,
No need for alarm,
It only hums,
It doesn't harm.
▪▪▪▪▪▪▪▪▪▪▪▪▪▪▪▪▪▪▪▪▪▪▪▪

Tie a knot, tie a knot.
Tie a tight, tight knot.
Tie a knot in the shape of a nought.
▪▪▪▪▪▪▪▪▪▪▪▪▪▪▪▪▪▪▪▪▪▪▪▪

Red blood, green blood.
(x3)
▪▪▪▪▪▪▪▪▪▪▪▪▪▪▪▪▪▪▪▪▪▪▪▪

I'm a sheet slitter.
I slit sheets.
I'm the sleekest sheet slitter that ever slit sheets.
▪▪▪▪▪▪▪▪▪▪▪▪▪▪▪▪▪▪▪▪▪▪▪▪

Tongue Twisters

Busy buzzing bumble bees. (x3)

∎∎∎∎∎∎∎∎∎∎∎∎∎∎∎∎∎∎∎∎∎∎∎

A lump of red leather, a red leather lump.

∎∎∎∎∎∎∎∎∎∎∎∎∎∎∎∎∎∎∎∎∎∎∎

Nat the bat swat at Matt the gnat.

∎∎∎∎∎∎∎∎∎∎∎∎∎∎∎∎∎∎∎∎∎∎∎

I shot the city sheriff.
I shot the city sheriff.
I shot the city sheriff.

∎∎∎∎∎∎∎∎∎∎∎∎∎∎∎∎∎∎∎∎∎∎∎

A lady sees a pot-mender at work at his barrow in the street.
"Are you copper-bottoming 'em, man?"
"No, I'm aluminiuming 'em, Mam."

∎∎∎∎∎∎∎∎∎∎∎∎∎∎∎∎∎∎∎∎∎∎∎

I am not a pheasant plucker, I'm a pheasant plucker's son but I'll be plucking pheasants when the pheasant plucker's gone.

∎∎∎∎∎∎∎∎∎∎∎∎∎∎∎∎∎∎∎∎∎∎∎

-Suzie, Suzie, working in a shoeshine shop.
All day long she sits and shines,
all day long she shines and sits, and sits and shines, and shines and sits, and sits and shines, and shines and sits.
Suzie, Suzie, working in a shoeshine shop.

-Tommy, Tommy, toiling in a tailor's shop.
All day long he fits and tucks,
all day long he tucks and fits,
and fits and tucks, and tucks and fits,
and fits and tucks, and tucks and fits.
Tommy, Tommy, toiling in a tailor's shop.

∎∎∎∎∎∎∎∎∎∎∎∎∎∎∎∎∎∎∎∎∎∎∎

Preshrunk silk shirts. (x3)

∎∎∎∎∎∎∎∎∎∎∎∎∎∎∎∎∎∎∎∎∎∎∎

Craig Quinn's quick trip to Crabtree Creek.

* * *

Six shining cities, six shining cities, six shining cities.

* * *

While we were walking, we were watching window washers wash Washington's windows with warm washing water.

* * *

A big black bear sat on a big black bug.

* * *

A bloke's bike back brake block broke.

* * *

Sweet sagacious Sally Sanders said she sure saw seven segregated seaplanes sailing swiftly southward Saturday.

* * *

Betty Botter bought some butter but, said she, the butter's bitter.
If I put it in my batter, it will make my batter bitter.
But a bit of better butter will make my bitter batter better.
So she bought some better butter, better than the bitter butter,
put it in her bitter batter, made her bitter batter better.
So it was better Betty Botter bought some better butter.

* * *

How much oil boil can a gum boil boil if a gum boil can boil oil?

* * *

Good blood, bad blood, good blood, bad blood, good blood, bad blood.

* * *

No nose knows like a gnome's nose knows.

* * *

Freshly fried fresh flesh. (x3)

* * *

Tongue Twisters

There are two minutes difference from four to two to two to two, from two to two to two, too.

There once was a man who had a sister, his name was Mr. Fister. Mr. Fister's sister sold sea shells by the sea shore. Mr. Fister didn't sell sea shells, he sold silk sheets. Mr. Fister told his sister that he sold six silk sheets to six shieks. The sister of Mr. Fister said I sold six shells to six shieks too!
■■■■■■■■■■■■■■■■■■■■■■■

Sally sells sea shells by the sea shore. But if Sally sells sea shells by the sea shore then where are the sea shells Sally sells?
■■■■■■■■■■■■■■■■■■■■■■■

She stood on the steps of Burgess's Fish Sauce Shop, mimicking him hiccuping and amicably welcoming him in.
■■■■■■■■■■■■■■■■■■■■■■■

Swan swam over the sea.
Swim, swan, swim!
Swan swam back again.
Well swum swan!
■■■■■■■■■■■■■■■■■■■■■■■

Sally is a sheet slitter, she slits sheets.
■■■■■■■■■■■■■■■■■■■■■■■

She sells sea shells on the sea shore;
The shells that she sells are sea shells I'm sure.
So if she sells sea shells on the sea shore,
I'm sure that the shells are sea shore shells.
■■■■■■■■■■■■■■■■■■■■■■■

You know New York.
You need New York.
You know you need unique New York.
■■■■■■■■■■■■■■■■■■■■■■■

What noise annoys an oyster most?
A noisy noise annoys an oyster most.
■■■■■■■■■■■■■■■■■■■■■■■

Adam Smith

Ripe white wheat reapers reap ripe white wheat right.
••••••••••••••••••••••••

I see a sea down by the seashore.
But which sea do you see down by the seashore?
••••••••••••••••••••••••

Old Mr. Hunt had a cuddy punt
Not a cuddy punt
but a hunt punt cuddy.
••••••••••••••••••••••••

As one black bug, bled blue, black blood. The other black bug bled blue.
••••••••••••••••••••••••

Mommy made me eat my M&Ms.
••••••••••••••••••••••••

I'm not the fig plucker,
nor the fig plucker's son,
but I'll pluck figs
till the fig plucker comes.
••••••••••••••••••••••••

A gazillion gigantic grapes gushed gradually giving gophers gooey guts.
••••••••••••••••••••••••

Aluminum, linoleum, molybdenum, aluminum, linoleum, molybdenum, aluminum, linoleum, molybdenum.
••••••••••••••••••••••••

Thin grippy thick slippery.
(x3)
••••••••••••••••••••••••

A tree toad loved a she-toad,
Who lived up in a tree.
He was a three-toed tree toad,
But a two-toed toad was she.
The three-toed tree toad tried to win,
The two-toed she-toad's heart,
For the three-toed tree toad loved the ground,

Tongue Twisters

That the two-toed tree toad trod.
But the three-toed tree toad tried in vain.
He couldn't please her whim.
From her tree toad bower,
With her two-toed power,
The she-toad vetoed him.

- - -

The owner of the inside inn was inside his inside inn with his inside outside his inside inn.

- - -

If you notice this notice, you will notice that this notice is not worth noticing.

- - -

If you understand, say "understand".
If you don't understand, say "don't understand".
But if you understand and say "don't understand".
How do I understand that you understand.

Understand!?

- - -

She sees cheese. (x3)

- - -

Brent Spence Bridge.
Clay Wade Bailey Bridge.
There those thousand thinkers were thinking where did those other three thieves go through.

- - -

Five frantic frogs fled from fifty fierce fishes.

- - -

One smart fellow, he felt smart.
Two smart fellows, they felt smart.
Three smart fellows, they felt smart.
Four smart fellows, they felt smart.
Five smart fellows, they felt smart.
Six smart fellows, they felt smart.

- - -

Adam Smith

Seven sleazy shysters in sharkskin suits sold sheared sealskins to seasick sailors.
▪▪▪▪▪▪▪▪▪▪▪▪▪▪▪▪▪▪▪▪▪

I would if I could! But I can't, so I won't!
▪▪▪▪▪▪▪▪▪▪▪▪▪▪▪▪▪▪▪▪▪

What a to do to die today,
At a quarter or two to two.
A terrible difficult thing to say,
But a harder thing still to do.
The dragon will come at the beat of the drum,
With a rat-a-tat-tat a-tat-tat a-tat-to.
At a quarter or two to two today,
At a quarter or two to two.
▪▪▪▪▪▪▪▪▪▪▪▪▪▪▪▪▪▪▪▪▪

Love's a feeling you feel when you feel you're going to feel the feeling you've never felt before.
▪▪▪▪▪▪▪▪▪▪▪▪▪▪▪▪▪▪▪▪▪

Silly sheep weep and sleep. (x3)
▪▪▪▪▪▪▪▪▪▪▪▪▪▪▪▪▪▪▪▪▪

Truly rural,
truly rural,
truly rural.
▪▪▪▪▪▪▪▪▪▪▪▪▪▪▪▪▪▪▪▪▪

A turbot's not a burbot, for a turbot's a butt, but a burbot's not.
▪▪▪▪▪▪▪▪▪▪▪▪▪▪▪▪▪▪▪▪▪

I know a boy named Tate who dined with his girl at eight eight.
I'm unable to state what Tate ate at eight eight or what Tate's tête à tête ate at eight eight.

The seething sea ceaseth; thus the seething sea sufficeth us.
▪▪▪▪▪▪▪▪▪▪▪▪▪▪▪▪▪▪▪▪▪

Real weird rear wheels. (x3)
▪▪▪▪▪▪▪▪▪▪▪▪▪▪▪▪▪▪▪▪▪

I slit a sheet,
a sheet I slit,
▪▪▪▪▪▪▪▪▪▪▪▪▪▪▪▪▪▪▪▪▪

Tongue Twisters

upon a slitted sheet I sit.
....

A pessimistic pest exists amidst us. (x3)
....

Knife and a fork bottle and a cork that is the way you spell New York.
Chicken in the car and the car can go, that is the way you spell Chicago.
....

Five fuzzy French frogs Frolicked through the fields in France.
....

Two to two to Toulouse? (x3)
....

Swatch watch. (x3)
....

Dr. Johnson and Mr. Johnson, after great consideration, came to the conclusion that the Indian nation beyond the Indian Ocean is back in education because the chief occupation is cultivation.
....

Round and round the rugged rock the ragged rascal ran.
....

Buckets of bug blood, buckets of bug blood, buckets of bug blood
....

I'm a sock cutter and I cut socks.
I'm a sock cutter and I cut socks.
I'm a sock cutter and I cut socks.
....

If coloured caterpillars could change their colours constantly could they keep their coloured coat coloured properly?
....

We won,
we won,
....

we won,
we won.

▪▪▪▪▪▪▪▪▪▪▪▪▪▪▪▪▪▪▪▪▪▪▪▪

Thirty-three thousand people think that Thursday is their thirtieth birthday.

How may saws could a see-saw saw if a see-saw could saw saws?

▪▪▪▪▪▪▪▪▪▪▪▪▪▪▪▪▪▪▪▪▪▪▪▪

As he gobbled the cakes on his plate, the greedy ape said as he ate, the greener green grapes are, the keener keen apes are to gobble green grape cakes, they're great!

▪▪▪▪▪▪▪▪▪▪▪▪▪▪▪▪▪▪▪▪▪▪▪▪

How much myrtle would a wood turtle hurdle if a wood turtle could hurdle myrtle?
A wood turtle would hurdle as much myrtle as a wood turtle could hurdle if a wood turtle could hurdle myrtle.

▪▪▪▪▪▪▪▪▪▪▪▪▪▪▪▪▪▪▪▪▪▪▪▪

Shut up the shutters and sit in the shop.

▪▪▪▪▪▪▪▪▪▪▪▪▪▪▪▪▪▪▪▪▪▪▪▪

Rattle your bottles in Rollocks' van. (x3)

▪▪▪▪▪▪▪▪▪▪▪▪▪▪▪▪▪▪▪▪▪▪▪▪

A fly and flea flew into a flue, said the fly to the flea 'what shall we do?'
'let us fly' said the flea, said the fly 'shall we flee', so they flew through a flaw in the flue.

▪▪▪▪▪▪▪▪▪▪▪▪▪▪▪▪▪▪▪▪▪▪▪▪

How much dew does a dewdrop drop,
If dewdrops do drop dew?
They do drop, they do,
As do dewdrops drop,
If dewdrops do drop dew.

▪▪▪▪▪▪▪▪▪▪▪▪▪▪▪▪▪▪▪▪▪▪▪▪

If Kantie can tie a tie and untie a tie, why can't I tie a tie and untie a tie like Kantie can.

He threw three free throws. (x3)

▪▪▪▪▪▪▪▪▪▪▪▪▪▪▪▪▪▪▪▪▪▪▪▪

Tongue Twisters

Fresh French fried fly fritters. (x3)

∙∙∙∙∙∙∙∙∙∙∙∙∙∙∙∙∙∙∙∙∙∙∙∙

Gig whip,
gig whip,
gig whip.

∙∙∙∙∙∙∙∙∙∙∙∙∙∙∙∙∙∙∙∙∙∙∙∙

I was born on a pirate ship.
*(say it while holding your tongue)

∙∙∙∙∙∙∙∙∙∙∙∙∙∙∙∙∙∙∙∙∙∙∙∙

2 Y's U R.
2 Y's U B.
I C U R.
2 Y's 4 me!

∙∙∙∙∙∙∙∙∙∙∙∙∙∙∙∙∙∙∙∙∙∙∙∙

Little Mike left his bike like Tike at Spike's.

∙∙∙∙∙∙∙∙∙∙∙∙∙∙∙∙∙∙∙∙∙∙∙∙

Eddie edited it. (x3)

∙∙∙∙∙∙∙∙∙∙∙∙∙∙∙∙∙∙∙∙∙∙∙∙

Yellow butter, purple jelly, red jam, black bread.
Spread it thick, say it quick!
Yellow butter, purple jelly, red jam, black bread.
Spread it thicker, say it quicker!
Yellow butter, purple jelly, red jam, black bread.
Don't eat with your mouth full.

∙∙∙∙∙∙∙∙∙∙∙∙∙∙∙∙∙∙∙∙∙∙∙∙

Wow, race winners really want red wine right away!

∙∙∙∙∙∙∙∙∙∙∙∙∙∙∙∙∙∙∙∙∙∙∙∙

The ruddy widow really wants ripe watermelon and red roses when winter arrives.

∙∙∙∙∙∙∙∙∙∙∙∙∙∙∙∙∙∙∙∙∙∙∙∙

I'll chew and chew until my jaws drop.

∙∙∙∙∙∙∙∙∙∙∙∙∙∙∙∙∙∙∙∙∙∙∙∙

Triple Dickle. (x3)

∙∙∙∙∙∙∙∙∙∙∙∙∙∙∙∙∙∙∙∙∙∙∙∙

How many sheets could a sheet slitter slit if a sheet slitter could slit sheets?

∙∙∙∙∙∙∙∙∙∙∙∙∙∙∙∙∙∙∙∙∙∙∙∙

Supposed to be

pistachio,
supposed to be pistachio,
supposed to be pistachio.
■■■■■■■■■■■■■■■■■■■■■■

Chester Cheetah chews a chunk of cheep cheddar cheese.
■■■■■■■■■■■■■■■■■■■■■■

Real rock wall,
real rock wall,
real rock wall.
■■■■■■■■■■■■■■■■■■■■■■

Argyle Gargoyle
■■■■■■■■■■■■■■■■■■■■■■

Peggy Babcock,
Peggy Babcock,
Peggy Babcock.
■■■■■■■■■■■■■■■■■■■■■■

If you're keen on stunning kites and cunning stunts, buy a cunning stunning stunt kite.
■■■■■■■■■■■■■■■■■■■■■■

Two tiny tigers take two taxis to town.
■■■■■■■■■■■■■■■■■■■■■■

Sounding by sound is a sound method of sounding sounds.
■■■■■■■■■■■■■■■■■■■■■■

Willie's really weary. (x3)

Yally Bally had a jolly golliwog. Feeling folly, Yally Bally Bought his jolly golli' a dollie made of holly! The golli', feeling jolly, named the holly dollie, Polly. So Yally Bally's jolly golli's holly dollie Polly's also jolly!
■■■■■■■■■■■■■■■■■■■■■■

Out in the pasture the nature watcher watches the catcher. While the catcher watches the pitcher who pitches the balls. Whether the temperature's up or whether the temperature's down, the nature watcher, the catcher and the pitcher are always around. The pitcher pitches, the catcher catches and the watcher watches. So

Tongue Twisters

whether the temperature's rises or whether the temperature falls the nature watcher just watches the catcher who's watching the pitcher who's watching the balls.

∎∎∎∎∎∎∎∎∎∎∎∎∎∎∎∎∎∎∎∎∎∎∎

Tommy Tucker tried to tie Tammy's Turtles tie.

∎∎∎∎∎∎∎∎∎∎∎∎∎∎∎∎∎∎∎∎∎∎∎

John, where Peter had had "had had", had had "had"; "had had" had had his master's approval.

∎∎∎∎∎∎∎∎∎∎∎∎∎∎∎∎∎∎∎∎∎∎∎

Excited executioner exercising his excising powers excessively.

∎∎∎∎∎∎∎∎∎∎∎∎∎∎∎∎∎∎∎∎∎∎∎

Pail of ale aiding ailing Al's travails.

∎∎∎∎∎∎∎∎∎∎∎∎∎∎∎∎∎∎∎∎∎∎∎

Double bubble gum, bubbles double. (x3)

∎∎∎∎∎∎∎∎∎∎∎∎∎∎∎∎∎∎∎∎∎∎∎

If you can't can any candy can, how many candy cans can a candy canner can if he can can candy cans?

Octopus ocular optics. (x3)

∎∎∎∎∎∎∎∎∎∎∎∎∎∎∎∎∎∎∎∎∎∎∎

A cat snaps a rat's paxwax.

∎∎∎∎∎∎∎∎∎∎∎∎∎∎∎∎∎∎∎∎∎∎∎

This is the sixth zebra snoozing thoroughly.

∎∎∎∎∎∎∎∎∎∎∎∎∎∎∎∎∎∎∎∎∎∎∎

Salty broccoli,
salty broccoli,
salty broccoli .

∎∎∎∎∎∎∎∎∎∎∎∎∎∎∎∎∎∎∎∎∎∎∎

I saw Esau kissing Kate.
I saw Esau, he saw me, and she saw I saw Esau.

∎∎∎∎∎∎∎∎∎∎∎∎∎∎∎∎∎∎∎∎∎∎∎

A slimey snake slithered down the sandy sahara.

∎∎∎∎∎∎∎∎∎∎∎∎∎∎∎∎∎∎∎∎∎∎∎

Suzie Seaword's fish-sauce

shop sells unsifted thistles for thistle-sifters to sift.

▪▪▪▪▪▪▪▪▪▪▪▪▪▪▪▪▪▪▪▪▪▪▪

I eat eel while you peel eel

▪▪▪▪▪▪▪▪▪▪▪▪▪▪▪▪▪▪▪▪▪▪▪

Casual clothes are provisional for leisurely trips across Asia.

▪▪▪▪▪▪▪▪▪▪▪▪▪▪▪▪▪▪▪▪▪▪▪

East Fife Four, Forfar Five. (x3)

▪▪▪▪▪▪▪▪▪▪▪▪▪▪▪▪▪▪▪▪▪▪▪

Roy Wayne,
Roy Rogers,
Roy Rash.

▪▪▪▪▪▪▪▪▪▪▪▪▪▪▪▪▪▪▪▪▪▪▪

11 was a racehorse,
22 was 12,
1111 race,
22112.

▪▪▪▪▪▪▪▪▪▪▪▪▪▪▪▪▪▪▪▪▪▪▪

Wunwun was a racehorse, Tutu was one too. Wunwun won one race, Tutu won one too.

▪▪▪▪▪▪▪▪▪▪▪▪▪▪▪▪▪▪▪▪▪▪▪

It's not the cough that carries you off,
it's the coffin they carry you off in!

▪▪▪▪▪▪▪▪▪▪▪▪▪▪▪▪▪▪▪▪▪▪▪

She said she should sit. (x3)

▪▪▪▪▪▪▪▪▪▪▪▪▪▪▪▪▪▪▪▪▪▪▪

Mo mi mo me send me a toe,
Me me mo mi get me a mole,
Mo mi mo me send me a toe,
Fe me mo mi get me a mole,
Mister kister feet so sweet,
Mister kister where will I eat!?

▪▪▪▪▪▪▪▪▪▪▪▪▪▪▪▪▪▪▪▪▪▪▪

Will you, William?
Will you, William?
Will you, William?
Can't you, don't you, won't you, William?

▪▪▪▪▪▪▪▪▪▪▪▪▪▪▪▪▪▪▪▪▪▪▪

I wish you were a fish in my dish. (x3)

▪▪▪▪▪▪▪▪▪▪▪▪▪▪▪▪▪▪▪▪▪▪▪

Tongue Twisters

She stood on the balcony, inexplicably mimicking him hiccuping, and amicably welcoming him in.

■■■■■■■■■■■■■■■■■■■■■■

The big black bug bit the big black bear, but the big black bear bit the big black bug back!

■■■■■■■■■■■■■■■■■■■■■■

Dust is a disk's worst enemy.

■■■■■■■■■■■■■■■■■■■■■■

How much ground would a groundhog hog, if a groundhog could hog ground? A groundhog would hog all the ground he could hog, if a groundhog could hog ground.

■■■■■■■■■■■■■■■■■■■■■■

How much pot, could a pot roast roast, if a pot roast could roast pot.

■■■■■■■■■■■■■■■■■■■■■■

How much wood could Chuck Woods' woodchuck chuck, if Chuck Woods' woodchuck could and would chuck wood? If Chuck Woods' woodchuck could and would chuck wood, how much wood could and would Chuck Woods' woodchuck chuck? Chuck Woods' woodchuck would chuck, he would, as much as he could, and chuck as much wood as any woodchuck would, if a woodchuck could and would chuck wood.

■■■■■■■■■■■■■■■■■■■■■■

Mary Mac's mother's making Mary Mac marry me.
My mother's making me marry Mary Mac.
Will I always be so Merry when Mary's taking care of me?

Will I always be so merry when I marry Mary Mac?
∎∎∎∎∎∎∎∎∎∎∎∎∎∎∎∎∎∎∎∎∎

Mr. Tongue Twister tried to train his tongue to twist and turn, and twit a twat, to learn the letter "T".
∎∎∎∎∎∎∎∎∎∎∎∎∎∎∎∎∎∎∎∎∎

Pete's pa pet poked to the pea patch to pick a peck of peas for the poor pink pig in the pine hole pig-pen.
∎∎∎∎∎∎∎∎∎∎∎∎∎∎∎∎∎∎∎∎∎

She saw Sherif's shoes on the sofa. But was she so sure she saw Sherif's shoes on the sofa?

Through three cheese trees three free fleas flew.
While these fleas flew, freezy breeze blew.
Freezy breeze made these three trees freeze.
Freezy trees made these trees' cheese freeze.
That's what made these three free fleas sneeze.
∎∎∎∎∎∎∎∎∎∎∎∎∎∎∎∎∎∎∎∎∎

Two tried and true tridents. (x3)
∎∎∎∎∎∎∎∎∎∎∎∎∎∎∎∎∎∎∎∎∎

Rudder valve reversals. (x3)
∎∎∎∎∎∎∎∎∎∎∎∎∎∎∎∎∎∎∎∎∎

Birdie birdie in the sky laid a turdie in my eye.
If cows could fly I'd have a cow pie in my eye.
∎∎∎∎∎∎∎∎∎∎∎∎∎∎∎∎∎∎∎∎∎

How many cans can a cannibal nibble if a cannibal can nibble cans? As many cans as a cannibal can nibble if a cannibal can nibble cans.
∎∎∎∎∎∎∎∎∎∎∎∎∎∎∎∎∎∎∎∎∎

Thirty-three thirsty, thundering thoroughbreds thumped Mr. Thurber on Thursday.
∎∎∎∎∎∎∎∎∎∎∎∎∎∎∎∎∎∎∎∎∎

Four furious friends fought for the phone.
∎∎∎∎∎∎∎∎∎∎∎∎∎∎∎∎∎∎∎∎∎

Tongue Twisters

Plymouth sleuths thwart Luther's slithering.

▪▪▪▪▪▪▪▪▪▪▪▪▪▪▪▪▪▪▪▪▪▪

Bobby Bippy bought a bat.
Bobby Bippy bought a ball.
With his bat Bob banged the ball,
Banged it bump against the wall,
But so boldly Bobby banged it,
That he burst his rubber ball,
"Boo!" cried Bobby,
Bad luck ball,
Bad luck Bobby, bad luck ball,
Now to drown his many troubles,
Bobby Bippy's blowing bubbles.

▪▪▪▪▪▪▪▪▪▪▪▪▪▪▪▪▪▪▪▪▪▪

Black background, brown background. (x3)

▪▪▪▪▪▪▪▪▪▪▪▪▪▪▪▪▪▪▪▪▪▪

Why do you cry, Willy?
Why do you cry?
Why, Willy?
Why, Willy?
Why, Willy? Why?

Very well, very well, very well.

▪▪▪▪▪▪▪▪▪▪▪▪▪▪▪▪▪▪▪▪▪▪

Tie twine to three tree twigs.

▪▪▪▪▪▪▪▪▪▪▪▪▪▪▪▪▪▪▪▪▪▪

Rory the warrior and Roger the worrier were reared wrongly in a rural brewery.

▪▪▪▪▪▪▪▪▪▪▪▪▪▪▪▪▪▪▪▪▪▪

Mares eat oats and does eat oats, and little lambs eat ivy.
A Kid will eat ivy too, wouldn't ewe?

▪▪▪▪▪▪▪▪▪▪▪▪▪▪▪▪▪▪▪▪▪▪

Three short sword sheaths. (x3)

▪▪▪▪▪▪▪▪▪▪▪▪▪▪▪▪▪▪▪▪▪▪

Caution: Wide Right Turns. (x3)

▪▪▪▪▪▪▪▪▪▪▪▪▪▪▪▪▪▪▪▪▪▪

Adam Smith

Rolling red wagons. (x3)
∙∙∙∙∙∙∙∙∙∙∙∙∙∙∙∙∙∙∙∙∙∙∙

Green glass globes glow greenly.
∙∙∙∙∙∙∙∙∙∙∙∙∙∙∙∙∙∙∙∙∙∙∙

Robert Wayne Rutter. (x3)
∙∙∙∙∙∙∙∙∙∙∙∙∙∙∙∙∙∙∙∙∙∙∙

I stood sadly on the silver steps of Burgess's fish sauce shop, mimicking him hiccuping, and wildly welcoming him within.
∙∙∙∙∙∙∙∙∙∙∙∙∙∙∙∙∙∙∙∙∙∙∙

As I was in Arkansas I saw a saw that could out saw any saw I ever saw saw. If you happen to be in Arkansas and see a saw that can out saw the saw I saw saw I'd like to see the saw you saw saw.
∙∙∙∙∙∙∙∙∙∙∙∙∙∙∙∙∙∙∙∙∙∙∙

Black back bat. (x3)
∙∙∙∙∙∙∙∙∙∙∙∙∙∙∙∙∙∙∙∙∙∙∙

The queen in green screamed.
∙∙∙∙∙∙∙∙∙∙∙∙∙∙∙∙∙∙∙∙∙∙∙

How many berries could a bare berry carry, if a bare berry could carry berries?
Well they can't carry berries, (which could make you very wary), but a bare berry carried is more scary!
∙∙∙∙∙∙∙∙∙∙∙∙∙∙∙∙∙∙∙∙∙∙∙

What did you have for breakfast?
- rubber balls and liquor!
What did you have for lunch?
- rubber balls and liquor!
What did you have for dinner?
- rubber balls and liquor!
What do you do when your sister comes home?
- rubber balls and liquor!
∙∙∙∙∙∙∙∙∙∙∙∙∙∙∙∙∙∙∙∙∙∙∙

Snap Crackel pop,
Snap Crackel pop,
Snap Crackel pop
∙∙∙∙∙∙∙∙∙∙∙∙∙∙∙∙∙∙∙∙∙∙∙

Tongue Twisters

Six slimy snails sailed silently.

I thought, I thought of thinking of thanking you.

Seven slick slimey snakes slowly sliding southward.

Red Buick, blue Buick. (x3)

Roofs of mushrooms rarely mush too much.

He threw three balls.

The great Greek grape growers grow great Greek grapes.

Singing Sammy sung songs on sinking sand.

We're real rear wheels. (x3)

Rhys watched Ross switch his Irish wristwatch for a Swiss wristwatch.

I wish to wash my Irish wristwatch.

Near an ear, a nearer ear, a nearly eerie ear.

On a lazy laser raiser lies a laser ray eraser.

Scissors sizzle, thistles sizzle. (x3)

Tom threw Tim three thumbtacks.

How much caramel can a canny canonball cram in a camel if a canny canonball can cram caramel in a camel?

I saw Susie sitting in a shoe shine shop.
Where she sits she shines, and where she shines she sits.

How many boards,
Could the Mongols hoard,
If the Mongol hordes got bored?

How can a clam cram in a clean cream can?

Send toast to ten tense stout saints' ten tall tents.

Denise sees the fleece,
Denise sees the fleas.
At least Denise could sneeze
and feed and freeze the fleas.

Coy knows pseudonoise codes.

Sheena leads, Sheila needs. (x3)

The thirty-three thieves thought that they thrilled the throne throughout Thursday.

Something in a thirty-acre thermal thicket of thorns and thistles thumped and thundered threatening the three-D thoughts of Matthew the thug - although, theatrically, it was only the thirteen-thousand thistles and thorns through the underneath of his thigh that the thirty year old thug thought of that morning.

Can you can a can as a canner can can a can?

Seth at Sainsbury's sells

Tongue Twisters

thick socks.
....

You cuss, I cuss, we all cuss, for asparagus!
....

Roberta ran rings around the Roman ruins.
....

Clean clams crammed in clean cans.
....

Six sick hicks nick six slick bricks with picks and sticks.
....

I wish to wish the wish you wish to wish, but if you wish the wish the witch wishes, I won't wish the wish you wish to wish.
....

Stupid superstition! (x3)
....

There was a fisherman named Fisher who fished for some fish in a fissure. Till a fish with a grin, pulled the fisherman in. Now they're fishing the fissure for Fisher.
....

World Wide Web. (x3)
....

To sit in solemn silence in a dull, dark dock,
In a pestilential prison, with a life-long lock,
Awaiting the sensation of a short, sharp shock,
From a cheap and chippy chopper on a big black block!
To sit in solemn silence in a dull, dark dock,
In a pestilential prison, with a life-long lock,
Awaiting the sensation of a short, sharp shock,
From a cheap and chippy chopper on a big black block!
A dull, dark dock, a life-long lock,
A short, sharp shock, a big black block!
To sit in solemn silence in a

pestilential prison,
And awaiting the sensation
From a cheap and chippy chopper on a big black block!

••••••••••••••••••••••••

Picky people pick Peter Pan Peanut-Butter, 'tis the peanut-butter picky people pick.

••••••••••••••••••••••••

If Stu chews shoes, should Stu choose the shoes he chews?

••••••••••••••••••••••••

Luke Luck likes lakes.
Luke's duck likes lakes.
Luke Luck licks lakes.
Luck's duck licks lakes.
Duck takes licks in lakes Luke Luck likes.
Luke Luck takes licks in lakes duck likes.

••••••••••••••••••••••••

Seventy seven benevolent elephants. (x3)

••••••••••••••••••••••••

There those thousand thinkers were thinking how did the other three thieves go through.

••••••••••••••••••••••••

Santa's Short Suit Shrunk

••••••••••••••••••••••••

I was born on a pirate ship. (x3)

••••••••••••••••••••••••

Hold your tounge while saying it.

••••••••••••••••••••••••

I scream, you scream, we all scream for icecream!

••••••••••••••••••••••••

Wayne went to Wales to watch walruses.

••••••••••••••••••••••••

In 'ertford, 'ereford and 'ampshire, 'urricanes 'ardly Hever 'appen.

••••••••••••••••••••••••

One-one was a race horse.

Tongue Twisters

Two-two was one too.
One-one won one race.
Two-two won one too.

∎∎∎∎∎∎∎∎∎∎∎∎∎∎∎∎∎∎∎∎∎∎∎∎

Eleven benevolent elephants. (x3)

∎∎∎∎∎∎∎∎∎∎∎∎∎∎∎∎∎∎∎∎∎∎∎∎

Celibate celebrant, celibate celebrant, celibate celebrant.

∎∎∎∎∎∎∎∎∎∎∎∎∎∎∎∎∎∎∎∎∎∎∎∎

If Pickford's packers packed a packet of crisps would the packet of crisps that Pickford's packers packed survive for two and a half years?

∎∎∎∎∎∎∎∎∎∎∎∎∎∎∎∎∎∎∎∎∎∎∎∎

Six sleek swans swam swiftly southwards.

∎∎∎∎∎∎∎∎∎∎∎∎∎∎∎∎∎∎∎∎∎∎∎∎

Gobbling gorgoyles gobbled gobbling goblins.

∎∎∎∎∎∎∎∎∎∎∎∎∎∎∎∎∎∎∎∎∎∎∎∎

Did Dick Pickens prick his pinkie pickling cheap cling peaches in an inch of Pinch or framing his famed French finch photos?

∎∎∎∎∎∎∎∎∎∎∎∎∎∎∎∎∎∎∎∎∎∎∎∎

Pirates Private Property. (x3)

∎∎∎∎∎∎∎∎∎∎∎∎∎∎∎∎∎∎∎∎∎∎∎∎

What a terrible tongue twister,
what a terrible tongue twister,
what a terrible tongue twister...

∎∎∎∎∎∎∎∎∎∎∎∎∎∎∎∎∎∎∎∎∎∎∎∎

When you write copy you have the right to copyright the copy you write.

∎∎∎∎∎∎∎∎∎∎∎∎∎∎∎∎∎∎∎∎∎∎∎∎

A big black bug bit a big black dog on his big black nose!

∎∎∎∎∎∎∎∎∎∎∎∎∎∎∎∎∎∎∎∎∎∎∎∎

Elizabeth's birthday is on the third Thursday of this month.

∎∎∎∎∎∎∎∎∎∎∎∎∎∎∎∎∎∎∎∎∎∎∎∎

Ann and Andy's

anniversary is in April.
■■■■■■■■■■■■■■■■■■■■■

Flash message! (x3)
■■■■■■■■■■■■■■■■■■■■■

Frogfeet, flippers, swimfins. (x3)
■■■■■■■■■■■■■■■■■■■■■

Hassock hassock, black spotted hassock. Black spot on a black back of a black spotted hassock.
■■■■■■■■■■■■■■■■■■■■■

How many cookies could a good cook cook, If a good cook could cook cookies? A good cook could cook as much cookies as a good cook who could cook cookies.
■■■■■■■■■■■■■■■■■■■■■

Black block,
Black block,
Black block.

About the Author

Adam Smith is a comedian from USA (Chicago). His mission is to make people smile until their belly hurts. He has collected a vast collection of jokes and funny short stories that he wanted to share with entire world!

Thanks for reading!

Please add a short review on Amazon and let me know what you thought!

Thanks and good luck!
Adam Smith